Original title:
Candles Flicker in Frost

Copyright © 2024 Creative Arts Management OÜ
All rights reserved.

Author: Lorenzo Barrett
ISBN HARDBACK: 978-9916-94-456-1
ISBN PAPERBACK: 978-9916-94-457-8

Shimmering Hopes on a Winter's Eve

Under the stars, dreams softly glow,
Whispers of warmth in the chill below.
Hope flutters lightly, like snowflakes that fall,
Beneath the silver moon, glimmers call.

In the quiet night, hearts find their peace,
Melodies linger, offering sweet release.
Each breath a promise, a soft gentle sigh,
Carried on winds, as the cold night draws nigh.

Luminous Threads in the Fabric of Cold

Woven of starlight, the fabric is bright,
Threads interlaced with shimmering light.
In the tapestry dark, colors must blend,
Creating a warmth that begins to ascend.

With frosty fingers, we touch the divine,
The beauty of winter in each simple line.
Dreams stitched together, both fragile and bold,
Shimmering hopes in the fabric of cold.

Flickering Peace in the Heart of Frost

In the stillness of winter, peace takes its flight,
A flicker of warmth in the deepening night.
Crystals of ice, they shimmer and shine,
Each moment of solace, a treasure divine.

Gentle the whispers, the wind through the trees,
Songs of the night carried soft on the breeze.
Frost paints the world with a delicate hand,
Creating a vision so tender and grand.

A Glinting Warmth Amidst the Winter's Grasp

Amidst the cold, a warmth does remain,
Glinting like sunlight through soft falling rain.
Each heartbeat a lantern, guiding our way,
Through shadows of winter, into the day.

We gather together, a circle of light,
Facing the darkness with spirits so bright.
In the chill of the night, our souls intertwine,
Finding a glow that is purely divine.

Nurtured Sparks in the Depths of Winter

In the stillness, soft whispers glow,
Gentle warmth beneath the snow.
Each breath of life begins to surge,
As silent dreams within us emerge.

Crisp air carries a song so sweet,
Nature's rhythm, a steady beat.
Through the frost, our hearts ignite,
Nurtured sparks that chase the night.

Distant Lights in a Frosty Labyrinth

Wandering paths where shadows creep,
Hidden treasures, secrets keep.
A dance of stars on icy ground,
In this maze, lost dreams are found.

Whiffs of magic, mysteries play,
Guided by the lights, we stray.
Each turn reveals a story untold,
In chilled embrace, the heart grows bold.

Resonance of Fire and Ice

Where warmth meets the chill in sweet embrace,
Contrast unfolds in this sacred space.
Fires flicker with a gentle sigh,
While icy breath dares to fly.

A symphony of elements unite,
Melodies weave through day and night.
In the harmony, we find our place,
Resonance blooms in this timeless grace.

Ethereal Flickers in a Frozen World

In a realm where the crystals gleam,
Ethereal flickers dance and dream.
Soft glows shimmer on endless white,
Breath of magic, pure delight.

With each step, the silence sings,
Wrapped in winter's delicate wings.
In this frozen world, hearts align,
Finding warmth in a space so divine.

Ember's Embrace in the Frostbitten Night

In the stillness of the night,
Embers dance with gentle light,
Whispers soft, like a sigh,
Frosty breath beneath the sky.

Crimson sparks in icy air,
Warming hearts with tender care,
Silent wishes take their flight,
Ember's glow, our guiding light.

Glow Beneath the Snowy Canopy

Underneath the winter's shroud,
Softly covered, oh so proud,
Glowing dreams in layers deep,
Whispers of the night to keep.

Beneath the branches, gently sway,
Stars peek out, then fade away,
A cozy warmth, a hushed delight,
Glow beneath the snowy night.

Radiant Wishes on a Frigid Evening

Radiant wishes softly float,
Carried by the chilled night's coat,
Frosty winds, a gentle tease,
Whispers lost among the trees.

In this quiet, frozen space,
Hope ignites with a warm embrace,
As the moonlight paints the ground,
Radiant dreams in silence found.

Never Fading Light on a Cold Journey

Through the shadows, pathways wane,
Every step, a hint of pain,
Yet a light inside me glows,
Never fading as it grows.

Onward through the bitter chill,
Hope persists, a guiding thrill,
In the dark, I find my way,
Never fading, come what may.

Softly Shining in the Winter's Grip

Snowflakes dance in silver light,
Whispers of magic in the night.
Trees adorned in icy lace,
Nature holds a fleeting grace.

Moonbeams glimmer on the ground,
Silent beauty can be found.
Stars above, a twinkling crown,
Winter's peace spreads softly down.

Flickering Tales Beneath a Frosted Sky

Stories woven in the frost,
Treasures found, yet not embossed.
Crisp air carries tales so old,
In the night, their warmth unfolds.

Fires burn in hearts aglow,
Shadows dance in twilight's flow.
Each flicker tells a memory's flight,
Beneath the watchful, frosted night.

Luminescent Hues in Chilling Shadows

The world transforms in pale hue,
Colors burst, yet fade from view.
Winter's kiss leaves art divine,
Shadows merge with light's design.

In the dusk, the colors play,
Painting stories, come what may.
Every shade a soft embrace,
Fleeting moments time won't chase.

A Horizon of Light Amidst the Frosty Air

Morning breaks with gentle rays,
Chasing night in soft arrays.
Frosty breath on eager grass,
A world awakened, shadows pass.

Horizons blush with warming fire,
As the sun climbs ever higher.
Frosty air sings sweet and clear,
New beginnings drawing near.

The Last Glow of a Dimming Day

The sun dips low in a fiery blaze,
Casting shadows in twilight's haze.
Colors bleed in the evening air,
Whispers of dreams that linger there.

Birds retreat to their hidden nests,
As the world slows, taking its rest.
The horizon blushes, a fleeting show,
In the last glow of a dimming day's flow.

Radiance Amidst Winter's Grasp

Winter winds howl with icy breath,
The ground adorned in a shroud of death.
Yet from the cold, a warm light beams,
Radiance flickers, igniting dreams.

Beneath the snow, life quietly stirs,
Hidden treasures where the frost blurs.
Hope gleams bright through the frozen night,
A balm for hearts, a spark of light.

Gentle Flames on a Frigid Night

Softly the embers crackle and glow,
Casting warmth in the dark below.
Whispers of comfort in flickering light,
Gentle flames dance in the still of night.

Outside the world wears its chilly shroud,
Inside, we gather, happy and loud.
Our laughter weaves through the glowing sparks,
As love ignites in the quiet dark.

Illuminated Wishes Beneath the Ice

Stars twinkle bright in the midnight sky,
As frozen dreams beneath the ice lie.
Wishes float like lanterns in air,
Illuminated hopes that linger there.

The world is still, as if held in trance,
Each breath a soft, delicate dance.
Beneath the surface, a glow remains,
Whispers of futures, unbroken chains.

Flickering Lanterns in the Heart of Winter

In the still of night, soft glow ignites,
Lanterns flicker, casting dreams in light.
Snowflakes twirl, dancing through the air,
Whispers of warmth, forgotten cares bare.

Shadows play beneath the silver moon,
Each flicker sings a gentle tune.
Hearts embrace the chill, yet feel the fire,
In lantern's glow, we find our desire.

Ethereal Illuminations on Frosted Paths

Frozen pathways stretch, adorned with gleam,
Ethereal lights awaken every dream.
Footsteps crunch on a canvas of white,
Guided by stars that twinkle so bright.

A dance of frost, where shadows retreat,
Nature's embrace, so tender, so sweet.
Illuminations lead through the fray,
Carrying spirits, lighting the way.

Radiant Whispers on a Snow-Kissed Landscape

On a snow-kissed land, the silence speaks,
Radiant whispers flow through the peaks.
Each flake a kiss from a loving sky,
Gentle caresses as moments pass by.

In the hush of dusk, the world stands still,
Hearts come alive, filled with hope and thrill.
Under the blanket of soft, pure white,
We find our solace in the tranquil night.

The Warmth of Hope in the Chill of Night

In the darkness, shadows creep,
A flicker calls from dreams we keep.
Whispers of comfort softly flow,
A gentle reminder: hope can grow.

Stars above begin to gleam,
Guiding hearts through the frozen dream.
Each breath a promise, warm and bright,
Weaving courage in the night.

Glowing Hearths in a Frost-Nipped World

Fires crackle with tales untold,
Embers flicker, brave and bold.
Around the hearth, safe and sound,
In love and laughter, warmth is found.

Snowflakes dance like dreams unfurled,
While whispers wrap our tiny world.
Together here, we find our might,
In glowing hearths, dispelling night.

A Solace of Light Beneath the Icy Dome

Moonlight spills on fields of white,
A silver hue in the darkest night.
With every step, the world holds tight,
To glimmers of hope, serene and bright.

Under the dome, we gather near,
Sharing stories, joys, and fears.
In every shadow, solace bends,
As light embraces, our hearts mend.

Tranquil Luminescence in the Bitter Freeze

Frosty air wraps us in dreams,
As twilight paints on silent beams.
A tranquil glow on winter's face,
Brings warmth to every cold embrace.

In stillness, we find truth in light,
Soft luminescence through the night.
As stars alight, our spirits rise,
In bitter freeze, love never dies.

Echoes of Warmth in the Winter's Embrace

Whispers of fire flicker bright,
Casting shadows on snow's white.
The hearth sings with gentle cheer,
Echoes of warmth drawing near.

Each breath a cloud in the air,
Wrapped in blankets without a care.
Outside, the world wears icy lace,
Inside, it's a soft, warm space.

Luminescent Paths Through Frosted Woods

Stars dangle low in the midnight sky,
Illuminating paths where quiet sighs lie.
Frost paints the trees in silvery hues,
Nature breathes softly, the night to muse.

Each footfall crunches on powdered white,
Guided by moonsilver, a shimmering light.
Through winding trails, whispers reside,
In frosted woods, where secrets abide.

Faint Glows in the Winter Shadows

Hues of twilight in winter's shroud,
Faint glows break through the gathering cloud.
In distant corners where shadows dance,
A warm light flickers, sparking a chance.

Soft echoes of laughter drift in the night,
The warmth of the hearth a gentle delight.
In the hush of the world, we find our place,
In faint glows where winter's love leaves a trace.

Firelight Serenade on a Chilly Eve

Sparks rise high in the cool night air,
As firelight weaves a tender care.
Stories unfurl in the flickering glow,
Each ember holds memories we know.

Voices blend in a harmonious tune,
Under the watch of the silvery moon.
Embraced by warmth, we gather near,
In firelight's serenade, the heart feels clear.

Gentle Radiance in a Wintry Embrace

Amidst the snow, a soft glow plays,
Whispers of warmth in the cold days.
Trees wear coats of frosty white,
While stars above twinkle with delight.

In the stillness, hearts find peace,
Nature's beauty brings sweet release.
Each flake a story, brief but bright,
Crafting a canvas, pure and white.

As moonbeams dance on frosted ground,
A gentle touch, so profound.
Wrapped in silence, we find our way,
In wintry embrace, where spirits play.

With each breath, the world renews,
In the chill, love in hues.
Together we bask in this serene scene,
Gentle radiance, forever keen.

Serenity Illuminated on a Frosty Night

A quiet glow enfolds the night,
Stars above, a shimmering sight.
In the breath of winter's embrace,
Serenity finds its place.

Snowflakes drift on a gentle breeze,
Whispers of peace that aim to please.
Echoes of laughter softly ring,
In this stillness, our hearts sing.

Beneath the moon's watchful gaze,
The world transforms in a silver haze.
Footsteps muffled on the ground,
In silence, true beauty is found.

As nature sleeps, dreams take flight,
Serenity and peace unite.
In this frosty, enchanting night,
Hope ignites, forever bright.

Light's Embrace in the Chill of Dawn

Dawn breaks softly, a gentle sigh,
The world awakens, colors nigh.
Frosty breath hangs in the air,
As sunlight dances without a care.

Golden rays kiss the frozen grass,
In light's embrace, shadows pass.
Chill recedes, warmth starts to glow,
Nature's wonders begin to show.

Birds take flight in blushing light,
Songs of joy take to the height.
Every petal, every tree,
Awakens in this harmony.

In the dawn's quiet, hope unfurls,
Promises whisper in soft swirls.
Light's tender touch on a chilly morn,
Brings forth the beauty of a new dawn.

A Hearth's Whisper Beneath Snowflakes

In the glow of a crackling fire,
Whispers of warmth, we never tire.
Snowflakes dance outside the pane,
While inside, love softly reigns.

The hearth's glow is a tender guide,
Through wintry chills, we abide.
Wrapped in blankets, stories shared,
In this moment, hearts are bared.

Outside, the world is a glistening dream,
Softly wrapped in winter's seam.
But here, the warmth of laughter flows,
A heartbeat closer as friendship grows.

Underneath the starry skies,
A gentle peace, where comfort lies.
In every flicker, every sigh,
A hearth's whisper will never die.

Soft Gleam in the Depths of Winter

A flicker shines 'neath snow's embrace,
Whispers of warmth in a frozen space.
Quiet dreams in the frosty air,
Hope lingers gently, tender and rare.

Beneath the stillness, life stirs awake,
Each crystal bead a promise to make.
The sun peeks shyly, day unfolds,
Glimmers of gold through the chilly cold.

Melodies of Light in a Hushed Landscape

Soft notes drift as shadows play,
A gentle serenade, twilight's sway.
In the hush of dusk, colors gleam,
A symphony written in winter's dream.

The stars join in, a twinkling choir,
Echoing whispers, hearts inspire.
Moonlight dances on the purest white,
Casting sweet melodies into the night.

Fireflies of Warmth Against the Icy Canvas

Flickering lights in the frozen air,
Each one a spirit, bright and fair.
Warming the heart with a flick and glow,
Guiding the lost through the deepened snow.

In the stillness, they weave their song,
Reminding us where we belong.
A spark amidst the winter's chill,
Filling the night with a gentle thrill.

Sparkling Reflections on Winter's Ice

A mirror of glass beneath the trees,
Reflecting the skies, the whispers of breeze.
Each ray of sun, a brushstroke bright,
Painting the world with sheer delight.

Footprints trace journeys, stories unfold,
In the shimmering stillness, magic bold.
Beauty encased in the frosty air,
Holding the moment, precious and rare.

Radiant Breaths in the Frozen Silence

In the stillness of the night,
Whispers of frost take flight.
Moonlight dances on the snow,
Secrets of the cold winds flow.

Each breath a cloud in the chill,
Time halts, the world stands still.
A lantern glows in the dark,
Guiding us with a gentle spark.

Crystal stars twinkle bright,
Painting dreams in silver light.
We find solace in the freeze,
Nature's canvas, calm and pleased.

Echoes of warmth start to creep,
Into hearts where shadows sleep.
Radiant breaths in the air,
Embrace the silence, unaware.

Tender Flames Beneath Winter's Veil

Beneath the frost lies a fire,
A glow that sparks a quiet desire.
Golden embers wake the night,
In tender flames, all is right.

Snowflakes dance like falling stars,
Covering the world in silver bars.
Yet within us, warmth ignites,
Through frosty air, love unites.

Winter whispers, soft and low,
Hushed secrets that we both know.
Tender flames in the dark,
Igniting souls with a gentle spark.

As we sit with hearts aglow,
Outside the winds begin to blow.
Wrapped in warmth, we shall prevail,
Together, beneath winter's veil.

The Dance of Warmth in a Frozen Realm

In this realm of icy blue,
Where chill paints every view.
We sway as if in a trance,
Lost in winter's graceful dance.

Footsteps crunch on blankets white,
Fires crackle with delight.
With every twirl, the world shines,
In harmony, our hearts align.

Frosty tendrils in the air,
Yet inside, love's warmth lays bare.
Dancing shadows flicker bright,
Guided by the soft moonlight.

As snowflakes whirl in the storm,
We embrace the magic warm.
The dance of warmth shall prevail,
In this icy, wondrous tale.

Breaths of Light in an Icy Twilight

Twilight falls with a gentle sigh,
Colors blend in the frosty sky.
Breaths of light in every hue,
Painting the world anew.

The quiet whispers in the night,
Fill the air with soft delight.
Stars emerge from their slumber,
Bringing dreams we still remember.

Icicles gleam like crystal tears,
Reflecting all our hopes and fears.
Beneath the twilight, hearts ignite,
In this serene, enchanting light.

With every breath, we find our way,
Through icy paths where shadows play.
Breaths of light in soft embrace,
Guide us gently through this space.

Flickering Shadows Beneath the Stars

In fields where whispers softly tread,
Beneath the sky, where dreams are fed.
Shadows dance in twilight's embrace,
As stars awaken, filling space.

The moon's silver lights, a gentle guide,
Reveal the secrets time can't hide.
Ethereal forms, they weave and sway,
In the night's spell, lost and astray.

Crickets sing their lullabies sweet,
Echoing life, where night and day meet.
A tapestry painted in quiet hue,
Flickering shadows, a fleeting view.

Winter's Warmth in Glistening Light

The snowflakes fall, a silent choir,
Whispering tales of frost's desire.
In every flake, a story spun,
Winter's embrace has just begun.

The warmth of hearth, the crackling fire,
Draws us close, feeds the heart's desire.
With mugs of cocoa, laughter flows,
Through frosted windows, soft light glows.

Icicles form like crystal dreams,
Beneath the rays of sun that gleam.
A world transformed, pure and bright,
Winter's warmth, a wondrous sight.

Glimmers in the Icy Night

The stars above, they twinkle rare,
In icy realms, they cast their glare.
Glimmers dance on the frozen ground,
In this hush, pure magic is found.

Each breath a mist in the chilly air,
Nature's canvas, beyond compare.
Nights stretch long, with secrets to share,
Under the gaze of the moon's soft stare.

Crystals sparkle, a silent thrill,
Across the land, as time stands still.
A tapestry woven in dark and light,
Glimmers shine in the icy night.

Glow Against the Chilling Breeze

Amidst the chill, a fire burns bright,
With embers glowing, chasing the night.
Wrap me in warmth, this night to seize,
A dance with shadows against the breeze.

In winter's grasp, where frost might bite,
The heart finds solace, a flickering light.
Every gust whispers, tales of the past,
But here with you, the moments last.

With every glow, the world seems alive,
In the chilling breeze, our spirits thrive.
Together we stand, hearts open wide,
In the glow of warmth, forever tied.

Glowing Memories in the Frigid Air

In the quiet hours of night,
Whispers of laughter fill the chill.
Frosty breath, spirits take flight,
Captured moments, time stands still.

Footprints traced in glistening snow,
Stories held in the frozen ground.
Glowing memories start to flow,
In the silence, love is found.

The moonlight dances on the ice,
Casting shadows of dreams we knew.
Every twinkle, pure and nice,
Hints of warmth that we once drew.

As the chill grips the winter air,
Hearts are warmed by glimmering past.
In memories, we find our care,
A tender glow that holds us fast.

Flickers of Hope on Snowy Evenings

On snowy evenings, soft and bright,
A flicker sparks in the pale light.
Through the drifts, a promise glows,
As the frozen wind softly blows.

Each flake that falls, a wish we share,
Carried on winds, floating in air.
Beneath the stars, our hopes arise,
In winter's hush, dreams touch the skies.

From the hearth, the flames leap high,
Embers dance with a gentle sigh.
In every shadow, warmth is near,
Flickers of hope, we hold so dear.

Together we find joy in the storm,
Embracing the snow, a new norm.
In the cold, our spirits soar,
Flickers of hope forevermore.

The Glow of Comfort in a Frozen World

In the heart of the frosty night,
A glow emerges, warm and bright.
Cocooned in blankets, safe from the cold,
The stories of old begin to unfold.

Outside, the world is crisp and clear,
Yet inside, laughter fills the air.
With every hug, a soothing light,
Transforming darkness into delight.

Snowflakes whisper against the glass,
While time slips by, too swift to pass.
In the glow, we find our peace,
Comfort and love that never cease.

Now is the moment, held so tight,
In a frozen world, we shine bright.
Through winter's reach, our hearts will twirl,
The glow of comfort warms our world.

Radiance Wrapped in a Blanket of White

Beneath the blanket, soft and white,
Lies a radiance, pure and bright.
A world transformed, fresh and anew,
In layers of frost, dreams come true.

As the sun rises, glimmers shine,
Each breath we take intertwines.
Magic unfolds in the morning light,
Wrapped in warmth, a beautiful sight.

Children laugh, their joy unveiled,
With every snowball, friendship hailed.
In the crisp air, we find our way,
Radiance dances in silver play.

Together we walk through fields of white,
Hearts aglow in pure delight.
With each step, our spirits ignite,
Radiance wrapped in a blanket of white.

Light Breaths in the Frostbitten Air

Whispers dance on icy winds,
Underneath the pale gray skies,
Each breath a cloud of frosted dreams,
Every moment softly sighs.

Branches draped in crystal lace,
Nature's beauty, cold yet bright,
Shadows linger, gently trace,
The quiet glow of winter's light.

Footsteps crunch on frozen ground,
Echoes linger, softly fade,
In the silence, peace is found,
As the sun begins to wade.

Hope ignites in chilly hearts,
With every beam the dawn bestows,
Embers of warmth in coldest parts,
A quiet love, as stillness grows.

Silhouettes of Light Amidst the Snow

Moonlight spills on blankets white,
Casting shadows, graceful flow,
Figures dance in pale twilight,
A symphony of silent glow.

Trees like sentinels stand tall,
Guardians of the night so pure,
Listen close, hear nature's call,
Voices carried, soft and sure.

Footprints trace a story old,
In the depth of peaceful night,
Every step a tale retold,
In the silence, pure delight.

Flickering flames in distant sights,
Warmth and wonder in the cold,
Embers whisper of gentle nights,
As new dreams within us unfold.

Embered Hues in Frozen Whispers

Through the chill, soft colors gleam,
Nature's canvas, bold and bright,
Each brushstroke tells a winter's dream,
As day fades into velvet night.

Fires dance in hearts aglow,
Casting warmth on frosted skin,
Laughter echoes, soft and low,
In these moments, we begin.

Crimson hues and golden sights,
Merge with silver, soft and true,
In the magic of wintry nights,
We find the joy that feels like new.

Boundless beauty in the freeze,
Whispers linger, gentle care,
Embers spark a sweet unease,
As life breathes light in frozen air.

A Dream of Warm Light in the Darkness

When shadows stretch and daylight fades,
Hope ignites in hidden glades,
Each flicker turns the void to gold,
A heart's warmth breaking winter's hold.

Stars above like distant flames,
Illuminate our whispered claims,
In the quiet, soft and deep,
Light awakens from its sleep.

Dancing shadows, twisting light,
Guide us through the velvet night,
In every corner, warm and bright,
Dreams are born from dark's invite.

As dawn arrives with gentle grace,
We embrace this sacred space,
From darkness blooms a tender dawn,
In warm light, our fears are gone.

Glistening Flames of Resilience

In the heart of the night,
Where shadows dance and play,
A flicker ignites the dark,
Glistening flames hold sway.

Through storms that roar and rage,
They bend but do not break,
Each trial fuels their fire,
With strength they only make.

A warmth that never fades,
Clinging tight to dreams ahead,
With every ember glowing,
We rise where we once bled.

So sing, O brave reflectors,
Of courage fierce and bright,
In the place of despair,
Shine forth your steadfast light.

Shimmers of Hope in the Wintry Gloom

Amidst the muted white,
A sparkle waves from trees,
Each flake a whispered prayer,
Carried on the breeze.

When nights stretch on so long,
And hopes seem lost in shade,
The shimmers call us forth,
Through trials, unafraid.

They twinkle dreams anew,
Like stars in endless skies,
In every heart they bloom,
Opening our eyes.

So let the cold remind,
Of warmth that comes in time,
With every glimmer found,
We rise, and we will climb.

Embrace of Light Against the Cold

Against the biting chill,
A glow begins to form,
An embrace of gentle warmth,
A shelter safe from storm.

The dawn brings forth a glow,
That dances on the snow,
In its soft embrace we find,
The courage we must sow.

With every breath of life,
A flicker fills the air,
Light shines through all the dark,
A promise strong and rare.

Let go of winter's grip,
For spring is bound to come,
In the embrace of light,
We sing our joyous hum.

Flickers of Serenity in the Stillness

In the quiet of the night,
Where whispers softly blend,
Flickers of serenity,
Invite the heart to mend.

The moonlight gently falls,
On thoughts both near and far,
Each flicker tells a tale,
Guiding us like a star.

With each moment held tight,
A peace begins to grow,
In the calm of twilight,
Our souls begin to flow.

Find solace in the still,
Embrace the softest light,
For in those gentle flickers,
We find our path to flight.

Glimmers of Warmth Amidst the Ice

In frosted fields where shadows creep,
Small sparks of light begin to leap.
A whisper calls through bitter air,
With hope and fire, we find our flare.

Beneath the chill where silence lies,
The embers glow like distant skies.
With every breath, a flame ignites,
As hearts thaw gently in the nights.

Crystals gleam with radiant grace,
Reflecting warmth in nature's face.
Though winter's grasp may seem so tight,
We seek the glimmers, soft and bright.

Together we rise with the dawn,
Finding joy in winters drawn.
In all the cold, we hold the fire,
And kindle dreams that won't expire.

Shadows Dance with the Ember's Light

In flickering glow, the shadows sway,
As darkness twirls in a wild ballet.
Embers spark with stories untold,
Whispering secrets of brave and bold.

The night unfolds with a gentle kiss,
As light and shadow entwine in bliss.
Every flicker a tale to share,
In the woven depths of midnight air.

With every pulse, the fire sings,
Of olden times and simple things.
Wrapped in warmth, we lose our place,
In shadows' dance, we find our grace.

As moonlight glimmers on the scene,
We savor all that lies between.
A moment caught, a breath held tight,
In shadows' dance with ember's light.

Scented Luminescence Beneath a Starry Veil

Stars hang low like shimmering dew,
While night perfume drifts softly through.
A fragrance lingers, sweet and bright,
Illuminating the cloak of night.

Underneath the celestial glow,
A tapestry of dreams does flow.
Each scent a story from afar,
Binding us beneath every star.

In this embrace of night's perfume,
We dance in gardens that brightly bloom.
With every breath, the magic streams,
In scented whispers of our dreams.

The heavens call, a soothing hymn,
As midnight wraps its velvet trim.
With hearts alight, we claim our space,
In scented luminescence, we find grace.

Heartbeats of Light in the Bitter Cold

Amidst the frost, we stand entwined,
Where heartbeats forge a space defined.
Each pulse a beacon, warm and true,
Guiding us through the frozen blue.

In bitter winds, our spirits soar,
With every breath, we long for more.
Together we weave through icy nights,
Creating warmth, igniting lights.

With dreams held close, we brave the chill,
In shared laughter, we find our thrill.
As winter's grasp does fade away,
In heartbeats joined, we greet the day.

Through every moment, bond refined,
In the cold depths, our love aligned.
With hearts ablaze, we break the mold,
In cycles of warmth, against the cold.

Chasing Shadows Where Light Meets Ice

In the twilight glow, shadows dance,
Whispers of warmth in a fleeting trance.
Figures flicker, both near and far,
As night unfolds under a distant star.

Footsteps echo on the frozen ground,
Chasing dreams where silence is found.
Each breath a mist in the chilling air,
A fleeting moment, a secret to share.

Reflections twirl on the icy stream,
Merging shadows with a wistful dream.
The world a canvas of shadow and light,
In a harmony forged by the deepening night.

Where fragile glimmers meet the dark,
Every heartbeat ignites a spark.
Yet time slips by, an elusive sigh,
Chasing shadows as they pass us by.

Reflections of Warmth in Frigid Waters

Beneath the surface where coldness dwells,
Warmth is trapped in forgotten wells.
Ripples shimmer, revealing the past,
Echoes of laughter, memories cast.

In the stillness, whispers of grace,
Reflections flicker, a familiar face.
The icy depths hold stories untold,
Of love that blossomed in winters bold.

Each wave carries secrets, softly spoken,
Gentle currents where hearts are broken.
Yet through the frost, life finds a way,
In frigid waters, warmth will stay.

Through the layers, sunlight breaks free,
Creating constellations in the deep sea.
A dance of warmth within the chill,
Frigid waters, a testament of will.

Faint Glows in the Crystal Silence

In the crystal silence, faint glows appear,
Illuminating shadows that wander near.
Glistening edges where stillness lies,
A world transformed beneath the skies.

Moonlight shimmers on the frozen lake,
Creating pathways only dreamers awake.
Each sparkle holds a truth, a vow,
In the still air, remembering how.

The night wraps gently around the earth,
A lullaby sung to the dark's birth.
While faint glows beckon, inviting the heart,
Transforming solitude, a vibrant art.

In silence, a patchwork of light unfurls,
As the cosmos whispers, and time twirls.
Through crystal nights, hope's whispers sing,
In the depths of the dark, joy takes wing.

Ethereal Flames Against the Winter's Dark

Ethereal flames flicker in the night,
Chasing the darkness with radiant light.
Every flicker tells a story rare,
Of warmth ignited in the freezing air.

Beneath a canopy of stars so bright,
The world transforms in the glow's delight.
Crisp air hums with a vibrant song,
In this embrace where we all belong.

The fire dances, shadows come alive,
Chasing the cold, as spirits strive.
In the heart of winter, hope emerges,
As ethereal flames drown the surges.

Dreams are forged in the fire's glow,
In the depths of night, our spirits grow.
Ethereal warmth, a sacred spark,
Against the chill, we leave our mark.

Soft Flickers of Forgotten Dreams

In twilight's hush, shadows dance,
Where whispers of yesterdays prance.
Each flicker a story, gently told,
Of dreams that shimmer, of hopes that bold.

Beneath the moon's soft, silver light,
Forgotten wishes take flight at night.
They twine in the breeze, in the stillness found,
In the heart of the silence, where whispers abound.

Yet as dawn breaks, these dreams may wane,
Like dew on the grass, in morning's reign.
But in the heart's chamber, they softly stay,
Guiding the weary, lighting the way.

Luminescent Echoes in an Arctic Silence

In the vast ice, a stillness reigns,
Where whispers of frost dance in chains.
Beneath the stars, a shimmering glow,
Echoes of silence, where cold winds blow.

Here, time pauses, a frozen trance,
In the luminescence, dreams enhance.
Soft shadows flicker in pale moonlight,
Creating a canvas of infinite night.

Each breath is a story, caught on the freeze,
Echoing softly, like whispers of trees.
In the Arctic embrace, we find our peace,
In the quietest moments, our hearts release.

Dancing Flames on a Frosted Canvas

In a hearth's glow, warm embers play,
Dancing flames chase the chill away.
Each flicker brightens the frosted night,
A tapestry woven of warmth and light.

The crackling whispers tell tales anew,
Of joys remembered, of hearts that grew.
In the flickers, we see a story unfold,
Of love's embrace in the winter's cold.

Against the frost, the flames leap high,
Chasing away the shadows that lie.
On this canvas of night, we find our song,
In the dance of the flames where our dreams belong.

Whispers of Warmth in the Cold

In the heart of winter, where silence reigns,
Whispers of warmth break the cold chains.
A touch of kindness, a smile shared,
In the frost's embrace, love is declared.

Soft voices linger like echoes in snow,
Painting the silence, where feelings flow.
With every word, a flame ignites,
In the chill of the night, it sparks new sights.

Through biting winds, our spirits soar,
In the whispers of warmth, we long for more.
Together we face the frosty embrace,
In warmth, we find our save, our place.

Luminescent Echoes of Nostalgia

Whispers of dreams dance through time,
Fleeting shadows mark the climb.
Memories linger, soft and bright,
Echoes glow in the gentle night.

With every sigh, a story spun,
Moments captured, fading sun.
Fragments of laughter weave and twine,
In twilight's embrace, we intertwine.

A haunting tune, sweet and low,
Softly lit by the warmth we sow.
In the heart's library, we reside,
Illuminated by love's gentle guide.

In nostalgia's arms, we find our way,
Tracing paths where memories play.
Luminescent threads of the past,
In our soul's tapestry, forever cast.

Firelight and Frost: A Quiet Dialogue

In the hearth's glow, warmth ignites,
Chasing shadows through wintry nights.
Frosty whispers dance on the pane,
As firelight sings of love's refrain.

A tale unfolds in the crackling flame,
Each flicker recalls a cherished name.
Beneath the stillness of silver stars,
Hearts converse, erasing scars.

Candle flames flicker, soft and meek,
In the silence, two souls speak.
A dialogue forms, gentle and clear,
In the embrace of warmth, we draw near.

Firelight and frost, a perfect blend,
In this sanctuary, our hearts mend.
As warmth wraps around us tight,
Together we bask in the tender light.

The Light That Defies the Cold

Amidst the chill, a beacon glows,
In the dark, a courage grows.
Radiance flickers against the haze,
A promise of warmth amidst the craze.

Through icy breath and frosty air,
The light persists, a vibrant flare.
It dances boldly, a vivid thread,
Warming the path where angels tread.

Each flicker, a story yet untold,
Of fears conquered, and hearts made bold.
In the depths of winter's hold tight,
We find our strength in the softest light.

A defiance that glows, a spirit untamed,
In every heart, this fire we named.
Through storms we face, together we stand,
Guided by the light, hand in hand.

A Soft Candlelit Glow in the Arctic Stillness

In the arctic hush where shadows creep,
A candle's glow holds secrets deep.
Its gentle flicker, a tender sign,
Of warmth and solace, combined so fine.

Snowflakes drift like whispered dreams,
Framing the world in silver beams.
As the night settles, calm and slow,
The glow ignites the poignant snow.

With every flicker, a story weaves,
Of hearts that dance beneath the leaves.
In the stillness, together we find,
A flame that knows no bounds of time.

A soft light shimmers in the cold embrace,
Casting shadows, a delicate lace.
In the quiet of night, peace we bestow,
In the warmth of a candlelit glow.

Delicate Waxes Against the Frostbound Night

In darkness deep, the candles glow,
Their gentle flames a dance, a show.
Frosted breath upon the air,
Whispers linger, light and rare.

Shadows play upon the walls,
While time itself holds still, enthralls.
Beneath the starry canvas wide,
Hope and warmth in dreams abide.

Each flicker tells a story bright,
Of warmth that fights against the night.
In every waxen drip and sigh,
Resilience glows, it will not die.

So here we sit, as silence drapes,
In swirling thoughts, our spirit shapes.
Together, against the wintry chill,
We find our strength, we find our will.

Whispering Echoes of Light in the Snow

In the realm where silence reigns,
Snowflakes drift like soft refrains.
Whispers of light, a gentle chain,
Illuminate where dreams remain.

Each step taken leaves behind,
Echoes of thoughts, both pure and blind.
The world transforms, a canvas white,
Embracing shadows, claiming light.

Beneath the boughs where branches bend,
Nature's secret, hearts can mend.
In the hush, we breathe the grace,
Finding peace in this still space.

As moonlight spills on wintry ground,
In every corner, hope is found.
We dance with echoes, soft and slow,
In whispered dreams, the world will grow.

Infinitesimal Glow in a Frosty Slumber

In slumber deep, the world does lie,
A frosty breath beneath the sky.
Tiny sparks in every sigh,
Illuminate, like stars that fly.

Each moment pauses, frozen still,
In quietude, we sense the thrill.
Whispers drift through midnight's veil,
As slumber's tales begin to sail.

Frosted dreams like crystal lace,
In this serene and sacred space.
A glow so small, yet brilliantly bright,
Guiding us through the endless night.

We close our eyes, embrace the chill,
In frost's embrace, our hearts can fill.
For even in the darkest hour,
An infinitesimal glow holds power.

An Aura of Warmth in Chilling Dreams

In dreams we wander, soft and light,
Through realms adorned with twinkling night.
An aura blooms, a tender spark,
To guide us safely through the dark.

With every breath, a warmth ignites,
Defying cold with cozy sights.
As shadows dance on winter's breath,
We find the light that conquers death.

A laughter shared, a smile so bright,
Transforms the frost into delight.
In every heart, a flame can grow,
To chase away the chilling snow.

So hold this warmth, let it abide,
Through chilling dreams, let love be our guide.
For within the frost, we still can dream,
An aura of warmth, forever gleam.

A Warm Glint in the Chill of Night

Stars flicker softly, on velvet skies,
A touch of warmth where the darkness lies.
Moonlight dances, casting gentle beams,
Awakening whispers of midnight dreams.

Fires crackle beneath a starry glow,
Embers flicker, sharing tales of old.
In this embrace of a frigid night,
Hearts feel the warmth, igniting the light.

Each breath is visible, a ghostly plume,
Wrapped in the magic that banishes gloom.
Together we gather, as shadows play,
With voices entwined, we keep night at bay.

As dawn approaches, soft hues arise,
A warm glint shines from the waking skies.
In the chill of night, love's warmth ignites,
Creating memories that feel so right.

Light Hearts in the Grasp of Winter

Snowflakes tumble, a dazzling sight,
Embraced by frosty air, pure delight.
Laughter echoes in the crisp, cold air,
As light hearts dance without a care.

Footprints trailing where shadows meet,
Every step brings a joyful beat.
Scarves wrapped snug, cheeks rosy and bright,
Winter's charm holds us through the night.

Branches sparkle with nature's jewels,
Under the spell of seasonal rules.
The world feels fresh, a canvas so wide,
In winter's grasp, we find joy inside.

Even when storms howl, we stand strong,
With hearts alight, we carry along.
For every flake that falls in grace,
We find warm moments in winter's embrace.

Whispers of Flame in Winter's Breath

Crisp air wraps round in a delicate hug,
While whispers of flame offer warmth, snug.
Fireside tales spin like threads of gold,
Comforting stories in the winter cold.

Glowing embers sing as shadows sway,
Dancing softly, igniting the gray.
With every flicker, our hearts entwine,
Whispers of flame, in winter's design.

Outside the world wears its frosty attire,
Inside, the flame burns ever higher.
Together we share in this tender glow,
A sanctuary found from the world's snow.

Wrapped in blankets, with dreams shared anew,
Winter's breath cools, yet love stays true.
In the hush of night, we find our fight,
With whispers of flame, our spirits take flight.

Illuminated Dreams on Chilled Nights

Beneath a canopy of stars so bright,
Illuminated dreams escape into night.
The chill brings forth an inviting hush,
As nature holds its breath, in a gentle crush.

Frost on the windows paints stories unclear,
While hearts find solace when loved ones are near.
Each whispered promise hangs in the air,
In the delicate silence, we lay our care.

Moonbeams cast shadows that dance on the floor,
Each step brings echoes of memories stored.
In the calm of night, dreams take their flight,
Illuminating thoughts that flicker with light.

Time slows its pace, as stars softly gleam,
In the warmth of love, we share every dream.
On chilled nights, together we find,
Illuminated paths for hearts intertwined.

Veils of Light in a Snow-Covered Realm

Veils of light dance with grace,
Whispers of warmth in cold space.
Snowflakes fall in soft delight,
Wrapping the world in pure white.

Glistening paths where shadows play,
Nature's breath in shades of gray.
Every crystal, a story spun,
A symphony of peace begun.

In this realm where silence reigns,
Hope like winter gently gains.
A canvas vast, untouched, serene,
Dreams unfold in silver sheen.

As day breaks, hues softly blend,
A promise that will never end.
Veils of light and snow intertwine,
Creating magic by design.

Silent Harmony in a Frosty Haven

In the frosty haven's hold,
Secrets of winter, bright and bold.
Silent harmony fills the air,
Nature's artistry everywhere.

Icicles hanging with grace,
A fragile yet eternal face.
Branches draped in icy lace,
Time stands still in this embrace.

Footprints left on purest white,
Echoes of a fleeting flight.
Each breath a cloud of tender mist,
Moments cherished, not to be missed.

As twilight wraps the world in peace,
All worries and troubles cease.
Silent harmony whispers low,
In this haven, love can grow.

Spark and Sparkle in the Winter's Gleam

Stars descend from skies above,
Falling as winter's spark of love.
Each flake a whisper, a fleeting kiss,
In the night's chill, they dance in bliss.

Glistening paths of frosted light,
A magical wonder, pure delight.
Nature's gems in abundant grace,
Illuminate this quiet space.

As moonbeams weave through snowy trees,
A symphony played by the gentle breeze.
Every sparkle tells a tale,
Of warmth and joy that will prevail.

Hold close these moments, rare and bright,
In winter's gleam, all feels right.
Spark and sparkle in every scene,
A tranquil heart where you have been.

Calm Light in a Sea of Snowflakes

A sea of snowflakes, soft and light,
Blanketing the world in white.
Calm light filters through the trees,
Gentle whispers ride the breeze.

Each flake a journey, unique and free,
Woven together, a tapestry.
In the stillness, time softly drifts,
Carrying dreams on winter's gifts.

The world transforms in quiet awe,
Every detail enchants and draws.
Calm light dances on frozen streams,
Painting the landscape of our dreams.

As twilight falls, the stars ignite,
A serenade of purest light.
In this sea where beauty reigns,
Find your heart and ease your pains.

Milton Keynes UK
Ingram Content Group UK Ltd.
UKHW022341171124
451242UK00007B/84